DELIRIOUS WITH FEELING

Delirious with Feeling
Lianne M. Bernardo

First Printing: 2021

ISBN: 978-1-7750431-5-7

Note about the font: The font featured in the titles on both the book cover and at the start of each poem is based on my own penmanship (when writing in print).

To the man with the warm eyes and creative soul,
my rock star driving off to far-off places:
here is a time capsule of us.

૮.

Hello twice over:
to begin at the beginning
      again with some
      apprehension of repeated circles,
      mortifications unearthed...
And yet here we are.

(— "Maybe this time it is meant to be")

11.

And what shall I do
with you teasing words,
your mischievous smiles?
I knew you were trouble
the moment you hit reply.

lll.

What is this thread you're pulling,
this invisible tug
from your dexterous fingers,
your expressive hands?
These eyes have never seen,
never felt their touch
yet I'm reeled right in,
phantom whispers haunting my every step.

LV.

And what to do with
these golden words
you bestow upon me?
Like offerings they lie at my feet,
I know not what to do with them.

V.

I exalt
and yet I dread
for morn;
this could very well be
the best of dreams
or yet another false start.

VI.

Shall you gift me joy
or shall you bring me tears?
(—and what are you to me?)

VII.

What you've gifted
I cannot describe—
'Tis not poetry
or a mere thrill of laughter
against the starkness of life
but a blooming of some sort,
a plant of unknown variety
    sitting on my chest
flourishing onward and outward
      past my ribcage
        towards the sun.

VIII.

You've stolen something
from my lips

(I want it back)

(Or better yet
I'll take yours too)

LX.

Your eyes are anchors
pulling me in
hauling me
into your orbit;
I turn away but I
feel your gravity anyway,
inescapable,
all-consuming.

This passion may be
my end
(or yours)
(or ours)

X.

Standing tall, eyes locked:
who's falling faster,
you or I?

XL.

I find you lingering
beneath my skin,
in the folds of my brain,
reminiscent with the secret smile
plastered on my lips.

XLL.

With you
every worst-case scenario
evaporates without a trace,
every exit sign ignored;
it's only the here and now
and every happy thought in between.

XLLL.

These lips will burn of you
for days.

XLV.

Your touch,
your lips,
your taste
lingers;
I find I cannot rest.

XV.

Touch:
a dangerous weapon
comprised to
redirect our course.

XVI.

Long distances and divides
defines these spaces between us
and yet our words do not;
sturdy bridges they make,
binding our thoughts with
the time we bear.

XVll.

My lips unconsciously
seek yours
between those days we
do not meet.

XVlll.

I close my eyes
but sleep comes in snatches
like glimpses of falling stars
as my dreams seek your
soul, your person

(but you're miles
and miles away
while I'm still here)

XLX.

Sometimes love is but a dream,
a lofty cloud I could never reach.

And sometimes love is an arm's length away,
        reeling me in,
        layered on your lips.

XX.

Your eyes, they probe
and seek and rest
on my hair, on my lips,
settling deep into my eyes.

And I find myself
with no place to go,
nowhere to hide
but to melt further in,
forward and inward.

XXL.

These words
they lie inadequate
to the feelings they're meant to hold,
imperfect vessels
lacking the final touch.

XXLL.

And maybe for a moment
we'll speak the truth:
no silly words,
or joking refrains
to hold us back.

Maybe for a moment the
masks will slip,
the walls will falter,
and our hearts can breathe.

XXLLL.

Oceans away, wrapped by spires,
by harsh sounds and throngs
   of travelling souls
you remain not far from my mind.
All this history, all this beauty
cannot wholly distract me from
the weight of your eyes,
the attention of your mouth.

XXLV.

It's a fear:
to wake up and realise
all this fervour was
but a dream.

XXV.

It's dizzying,
this gravity you emit,
this pull I can't deny;
it knocks me out of orbit
until all I see are pink-tipped clouds
and all I've ever wished for
but a stone throw's away.

XXVl.

For all its newness
there is a calm,
a certainty to these words,
a solidness to these hands
I find I haven't seen before,
that I don't have the words
to match them with.

XXVLL.

Blanket me with little kisses
for nothing else will suffice.

XXVlll.

A furor and a stillness
under the same canopy—
How can this be?
An enigma storied in a bottle
dancing with lightning
and drifting with snow petals—
a precious gift in a
stark reality.

(—my thoughts with you)

XXLX.

There is a boldness to words
that is deemed necessary
and yet everything unspoken
is echoing loud and clear
with every touch and action.

XXX.

This isn't just poetry flowering
but something more,
something mysterious,
abstract yet tangible.

XXXL.

Easy now,
these coded symbols are no substitute
for your tender hands,
your mischievous lips,
the soulfulness of your eyes.

XXXLL.

You bring with you
not only the poetry of your soul
submerged in hidden depths
waiting to shore up when the tides draw back.

You also bring a calm heard
only beyond the clouds
in the silence of the heavens
the full moon cradled just above.

XXXLLL.

Mere hours are no longer enough:
I'm starting to want lifetimes too.

XXXLV.

You make it look easy
—the right words to say—
—the right moves to make—
as I bumble along
knocking every vase in the way.

XXXV.

Dizzying—
the whole world is a paradox
when we stand close to each other:
    —time stands still, time is never enough
    —passion and gentleness
    —everything and yet never enough
all these things collide
the moment we touch.

XXXVL.

I've gifted you bits and bobs,
little trinkets from around the world
but you've gifted me the whole universe
with your thoughts and questions
I've long forgotten,
dreams I've given up on many moons ago.

XXXVII.

And if you leave
take the stars with you
for I'll have no need of them.

XXXVLLL.

How secure it feels:
the brush of your hand
   at the small of my back,
the arc of your arm
   around my shoulders,
the resting of your gaze
   against mine.

XXXLX.

The taste of your lips,
the smell of your skin
the touch of your hand:
they linger in the spaces
    in between.

XL.

Hand outstretched
as though by reflex
but they catch only empty space,
your person absent beside me.

(—you should be here)

XLL.

For I'll let you weave your spell
with those nimble hands of yours
tracing my contours
like newfound land,
edges you and I never knew.

XLLL.

Never wholly alone:
you occupy my thoughts,
a singularity.

XLIII.

Cover me with your lips,
kisses of tempestuous storms,
of hidden flowers blooming.

Cover me with caresses,
soft touches made of reverent prayer
again and again.

XLV.

Each kiss more fervent than the last,
a field of flowers blooming in the night.

XLV.

You've unlocked something
in my blood, under my tongue:
my skin is not my own,
my lips, these hands, these thoughts
have lost all sense of
the passage of time.

XLVI.

I lay down words as forts,
demarcation of the land,
but they are all useless
against your soft hands,
roaming, searching at the earth.

XLVII.

These hands have found
but a taste of the cartography
of your skin.

XLVLLL.

We gather together
to dine at this table,
two enigmas out of place
against the great machine.

XLLX.

His fingers brush against my skin
like the strings on his guitar
writing a song against my soul
that only he and I can play,
every caress a note in time.

⌟.

He is calm where I am a storm,
his fancies like the wind where I stand like a rock,
free-spirited, free-minded
where I seek structure and order,
his singularity where I grasp at all the open straws.

(—what a pair we make)

22.

Standing at the precipice
between dropping the armour
or leaving the chestplate in place,
open my heart to the fall,
to the hurt, to the unknown.

lll.

Amidst this isolation,
this manufactured divide
as the world quivers and burns
I still feel your skin underneath my palms,
the curvature of your back,
the warmth of your lips against mine.

LLLL,

This distance is too cloying,
too palpable to bear;
your kisses, your touch,
the sound of your voice
is like some dream of long ago—
Remind me again how it goes.

LLV.

It's hard to stay cool,
it's hard to stay calm, collected, stoic
when there's a madness
running through my veins,
stoking the blood, incapacitating me;
your touch lingers along paths
you've traced on my skin,
ghosts that have made their home here.

LV.

I crave every detail of you
like something fierce,
something I can no longer describe.

LVL.

Hours, days chip away
since I've last felt your fingertips,
your lips brush against mine.
They're ghosts now,
these surfaces you've visited,
haunting my skin.

LULL.

Caught up in the whirlwind,
this fire dance of butterflies,
I forgot you had a knife.

LVIII.

My hands wish to grasp on
but it finds only empty spaces, the very air.
Fear is a trap
laying claim on full hearts
   of lofty dreams
   and warm feelings,
uncovering bare simple truths
and deep wishes.

                (Stay. Please stay.)

LLX.

I will write poetry of you
not with these words
but with my hands
(clumsy, wretched, scarred things they are),
with the trail of my eyes
(though they hide from your gaze),
from every single memory we've spun together.

↙X.

The fear is too ingrained:
you cannot see how much
you've become a part of me.

LXI.

I gift you words,
you gift me sunsets.

LXII.

My future, it seems,
   lies on your lips,
   the crook of your smile,
   the anchor that is your chest,
   in the warmth of your eyes.

(—things I dare not say out loud)

LXIII.

Your words are like
liquid honey,
its warmth covering
the distance:
    a condensation,
    a miracle,
    a heart roused alive.

LXLV.

Slip into my arms
and recognize my chaos:
mangled roots, unbidden thorns,
petaled rosebuds blooming upward.

LXV.

Innocent strung words perhaps not enough to
measure all the feelings poured forth,
poor substitutes to what I carry inside.

(—love letters)

LXVI.

Caro, you are poetry:
from the glimmer is your eye
to the curve of your lip,
the edges of your waist
to the melody on your fingertips
as you strum and tap in song.

LXVLL.

When dreams
are the only places
we can meet

(—lockdown romance)

LXVLLL.

Lose my thoughts,
lose myself,
in your oak-filled eyes.

LXLX.

Let us dream now, love,
of far-off places,
fresh grass to plant our roots.

LXX.

Do you know this?
That every time we part
you leave a little piece of you
behind with me:
    —a lingering touch on the arm,
    —a thoughtful word,
    —your taste in my mouth.

LXXL.

And when I least expect it
your taste blooms in my mouth
like autumn days
highlighted by an undercurrent
of unbridled passion,
flavours that are yours alone.

LXXLL.

Pockets of memory
side by side as we make
our way down open roads.
Unknown adventures await
with full hearts
and clear skies.

(—open roads)

LXXIII.

Shy heart:
I preserve the memory
   in stillness
   in a frame
and press it against my
chest, for my eyes only.

(—pressed flowers)

LXXLV.

How is it you save me from
these thoughts
when I least expect it?

LXXV.

I once gifted a man
a bouquet of my feelings
drawn together by my words.
He abandoned them,
fled into the recesses of himself,
with my heart left exposed on
    the cold floor.

For lesser men I would have gifted
mountains and valleys
and all the corners of this world.

But you, for you I would gift
every sunrise and sunset,
my heart underneath this rib cage,
bruised under this battered armour.

(if you want it)
(if you want me)

LXXVI.

These distances between us
need to close:
you're my visitor at dawn
and my wanderer at dusk,
unannounced in between.
I feel you next to me
but you ought to fill
that empty space.

LXXVLL.

Delighted and baffled,
ardent hopes that this
conversation never ends,
these kisses never cease
—on and on into eternity.

LXXVLLL.

Forgive me, I can be scared,
terrified to wake up
and find out you were
but a dream
a brief respite,
an illusion I fear I will
never recover from.

LXXLX.

If there seems to be
less words on this page
it is because the heart is balanced
but full (of you).

LXXX.

Writing love letters
for every day you're
not here.

LXXXL.

They say only you can save yourself
but in a way you saved me:
you reminded me of the
part of myself I've long forgotten,
trampled upon by the world at large.

I'm daring to dream again,
I'm daring to try again.

LXXXII.

Like shelter from the storms
raging outside
threatening to break in,
sweep oneself away
into the maelstrom,
swallowing you whole—
Your arms are a refuge
steadying me in place.

LXXXLLL.

Let me lay in
your arms
forever

(even as my earring
digs into your skin)

(even if I no longer
feel my arm)

LXXXV.

Thinking of all the kisses
I'll bestow on you
for every day we're apart.

LXXXV.

Will we and this
burgeoning love
conquer time?

LXXXVI.

My heart embraces
your heart
despite long distances
in between.

LXXXVII.

I found poetry again
   —in your words of encouragement,
   —in your hands as you hold me steady,
   —in your eyes seeking mine.

LXXXVlll.

Miles apart
divided by concrete and forest
yet a feeling remains
settled nicely within my chest
like warm arms embracing my heart
and mirth spreading across my lips.

(—feels like home)

LXXXIX.

This distance between us is palpable
counting down the days,
the hours,
until I'm in your arms again.

XC.

These soft bearings
always bring me back
to your instrument of devotion,
of a longing of steadfast desire.

XCI.

I'm ready
to drop this armour,
this heavy thing over my heart,
but I do not know where
to begin.

XCII.

This love operates under the sun
not at 4am with the cover of darkness.

XClll.

Did I conjure you
out of somewhere
out of nowhere
that you are right beside me now?

XCLV.

Swimming in these feelings
they populate the air around me
like a warm blanket,
a place I've always known.

XCV.

A gravitational pull,
a magnetic attraction,
the waves to the shore,
the wanderer coming home.

(—this is me to you)

XCVL.

Three little words
to encompass this entire
universe I'm feeling.

(—so why can't I say the words?)

XCVLL.

Where did you go
behind those shuttered lashes?
Retreated into your shell
where I can't reach you:
an aura, a shadow in
your soul's place I've never seen,
am not acquainted with.

XCVlll.

Come back to me,
rise up from the deep waters;
you've submerged yourself into
I can't see you in the dark.

XCLX.

Like water you drifted away
down the stream
that my anchor could
not capture, steady your plight.

C.

You left me without warning,
without any line of defense.

Now the bleeding won't stop.

CL.

I loved you
but it was too late.
I loved you
and you left anyway.

ell.

Maybe I'll remember the
good times with fondness
but right now they're a
field of landmines
I can't help but cross.

Cill.

Once your presence surrounded me
like a warm blanket:
secure, ever present...
Now I'm shivering in your absence,
the weight of the emptiness wearing me down.

CLV.

I can't bear to take down
these artefacts of you,
of us, just yet
even though the mere sight
of them makes me bleed more.

CV

Was it just a dream then—
us, our hands, the storms
we weathered, the open
roads we travelled?
Was the future all but a mirage?

CVL.

And now I'll never say it,
warn you from chasing
empty mirages in the sky.

CVII.

How could a heart so ablaze
turn so hollow?

CVIII.

He was water:
both invigorating
and drowning.

CLX.

You gave up
when there was still
so much love to be had.

CX.

And then your eyes flickered
out, you retreated—
I should've known then
you were letting me go.

(—hindsight 20/20)

CXL.

I didn't think
that night you held me
in your arms
that it would be the last.

CXLI.

I was falling deeper
whereas you were
eyeing the door.

CXLII.

I dropped the armour
low enough for you
to use the knife.

The bleeding's stopped
but I've lost much blood,
the wound still gaping,
patched up hastily.

CXLV.

You've ignited the dream
some lofty future involving
you and I
but you also doused it out,
leaving me alone on the life raft.

CXV.

And in the end I was
merely a wayward satellite
caught in his orbit,
his gravitational pull,
expelled forcefully and on
my lonesome way once more.

CXVl.

Loving you
was like anchoring
a cloud.

CXVLL.

I recited your name
like a prayer on my lips,
a mantra in the moment,
and forgot you were no
longer there.

CXVlll.

You heard the tears flow
and you did nothing.
I should have realized then
how closed your heart became.

CXLX.

One day I'll stop
trying to understand
why the passion died
and your heart went cold.

CXX.

One day I'll wake up
and you won't be the
first thing that
crossed my mind.

(—but not today)

CXXL.

Like taking a sledgehammer
to my heart
for falling too hard
and pouring it all.

(—where does that leave me?)

CXXLL.

With the coming of autumn
our passions changed
shifted colours:
but while mine infused into
   the roots of the tree
yours flowed to the tips
   of the leaves and fell.

CXXlll.

No photos of us,
only laughter,
moments in time
left in their place.

CXXLV.

Your absence lies heavy
on my back,
a weight I carry,
matching the hole you
left in my heart.

CXXV.

You left so few artefacts
in my waking life
but your fingerprints
are all over my memories.

CXXVI.

One day the gaping hole
you left me with
will fill with earth
and flowers will bloom
alive and flourishing
over the scar.

CXXVll.

Maybe it was meant to be
but only for a little while.

CXXVLLL.

When the dust settles
and the hurt heals
this is how I'll remember us:
driving down open country roads
under clear summer skies
happy, together, and free.

ABOUT THE AUTHOR

Lianne M. Bernardo is from Canada. She has previously written for high school and university publications, online e-zines, and Youth Speak News at the Catholic Register whilst accumulating a stack of unpublished content ranging from novel-length stories to poetry.

You can follow her on Instagram at *@shallibeapoetinstead*

ALSO BY THE AUTHOR

Shall I Be a Poet Instead?

Of Frost and Fury: Poems Written in the Land of Volcanoes and Giants

With Quiet Ardency

Scattered Stars

Overturned Cups

www.ingramcontent.com/pod-product-compliance
Lightning Source LLC
Chambersburg PA
CBHW032006040426
42448CB00006B/501